MATHS
MONSTERS
by **ZETA** MATHS

CfE Second Level
Book 2

Written by Michael Mackison & Caitlin Ferrie
Illustrations by Kirsty McAllister

© 2021 Michael Mackison
Published in 2021 by Zeta Maths Limited
Printed by Bell & Bain Ltd., Glasgow, UK

ISBN 978-1-915309-01-3

All rights reserved. No part of this publication may be reproduced, stored in a retrieval system, or transmitted in any form or by any means, electronic, mechanical photocopying, recording or otherwise, without prior written permission of the publishers. Any person who commits any unauthorised act in relation to this publication may be liable to criminal prosecution and civil claims for damages.

Illustrations © Kirsty McAllister 2021
www.kirstymca.co.uk

The right of Kirsty McAllister to be identified as the Illustrator of this Work has been asserted by her in accordance with the Copyright Designs and Patents Act 1988.

Acknowledgements:

The author would like to acknowledge and thank John Mowat for his invaluable contributions to the manuscript and editorial advice.

Also, special thanks to Hannah McGeogh for proofreading and checking the mathematical content.

In this book you will be practising… **Fractions**, **Decimals**, **Percentages**, **Algebra** and **Shape**

How to use this book

Complete **Day 1** exercise.

If you're stuck, see the website. QR codes link to videos.

Show all your **working**

Why? I can do it in my **head**!

It shows you **understand** what you are doing.

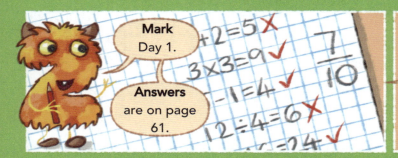

Mark Day 1.

Answers are on page 61.

Keep a **record** of your marks.

Use the **recording sheet** linked in the QR code.

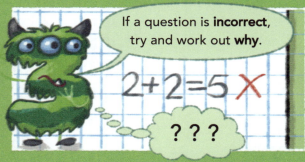

If a question is **incorrect**, try and work out **why**.

Check the **website**.

Or **ask someone** for help.

Complete the work for the rest of the **week**.

It should take **5-10 minutes** each day.

Work through the rest of the **book**.

Only do **one** exercise per day!

For more details, use this code.

Contents

		Page	✔
Week 1	Rounding to one and two decimal places	1	
Week 2	Place value	3	
Week 3	Addition of decimal numbers	5	
Week 4	Subtraction of decimal numbers	7	
Week 5	Mixed decimals questions	9	
Week 6	Mixed decimals questions	11	
Week 7	Multiplication & division of decimal numbers	13	
Week 8	Multiply decimals by multiples of 10, 100 and 1000	15	
Week 9	Divide decimals by multiples of 10, 100 and 1000	17	
Week 10	Fractions of a quantity	19	
Week 11	Fractions of a quantity	21	
Week 12	Mixed fractions questions	23	
Week 13	Mixed fractions questions	25	
Week 14	Fractions, decimals and percentages	27	
Week 15	Fractions, decimals and percentages	29	
Week 16	Percentages of a quantity	31	
Week 17	Percentages of a quantity	33	
Week 18	Fractions, decimals and percentages	35	
Week 19	Unit conversions	37	
Week 20	Simplifying expressions	39	
Week 21	Simplifying expressions	41	
Week 22	Solving equations	43	
Week 23	Solving equations	45	
Week 24	Solving equations	47	
Week 25	Patterns & sequences	49	
Week 26	Area & perimeter	51	
Week 27	Angles	53	
Week 28	Mixed exercise	55	
Week 29	Mixed exercise	57	
Week 30	Mixed exercise	59	

DAY 1

1. Round the following numbers to one decimal place:

(a) 7.13   (b) 2.75   (c) 1.47

(d) 2.49   (e) 63.86   (f) 29.89

2. Round the following numbers to two decimal places:

(a) 4.193   (b) 9.249   (c) 1.485

(d) 7.021   (e) 87.696   (f) 99.492

3. By rounding to the nearest pound, find an estimate for:

(a) $4 \times £6.31$ (b) $£7.78 \times 6$

(c) $12 \times £5.82$ (d) $£4.19 \times 7$

DAY 2

1. Round the following numbers to one decimal place:

(a) 17.35   (b) 8.93   (c) 63.86

(d) 58.39   (e) 27.94   (f) 142.99

2. Round the following numbers to two decimal places:

(a) 6.931   (b) 1.684   (c) 21.937

(d) 48.749   (e) 71.962   (f) 237.995

3. By rounding to the nearest pound, find an estimate for:

(a) $8 \times £2.85$ (b) $£8.61 \times 3$

(c) $40 \times £5.21$ (d) $£7.45 \times 10$

Week 1

DAY 3

1. Round the following numbers to one decimal place:

(a) 6.55   (b) 4.21   (c) 9.29

(d) 2.75   (e) 14.72   (f) 72.07

2. Round the following numbers to two decimal places:

(a) 2.760   (b) 0.839   (c) 15.725

(d) 52.724   (e) 0.709   (f) 121.236

3. By rounding to the nearest pound, find an estimate for:

(a) $8 \times £0.86$ (b) $£1.29 \times 4$

(c) $50 \times £4.89$ (d) $£9.99 \times 9$

DAY 4

1. Round the following numbers to one decimal place:

(a) 7.45   (b) 4.32   (c) 0.09

(d) 63.81   (e) 81.94   (f) 52.95

2. Round the following numbers to two decimal places:

(a) 9.801   (b) 4.288   (c) 21.455

(d) 8.247   (e) 101.193   (f) 89.999

3. By rounding to the nearest pound, find an estimate for:

(a) $5 \times £3.95$ (b) $£5.12 \times 6$

(c) $3 \times £14.89$ (d) $£2.94 \times 9$

Rounding to one and two decimal places   2

DAY 1

Write the value of the underlined number in words:

1. 8.4<u>1</u>7
2. 32.<u>7</u>19
3. 0.72<u>6</u>
4. 5.1<u>2</u>1
5. 45<u>1</u>.714
6. 89.<u>9</u>90
7. 104.37<u>5</u>0
8. 21.21<u>7</u>
9. 671.9<u>8</u>

DAY 2

Write the value of the underlined number in words

1. 1<u>2</u>.8
2. 93.1<u>5</u>9
3. 21.49<u>8</u>
4. 0.<u>3</u>1
5. 8<u>9</u>2.7
6. 9.<u>1</u>912
7. 31.4<u>7</u>2
8. 4.920<u>5</u>
9. 500.<u>3</u>

Week 2

DAY 3

Write the value of the underlined number in words

1. 87.**6**81

2. 2.92**2**

3. 1**1**6.91

4. 31.4**4**2

5. 98**9**.931

6. 82.52**6**

7. 5.27**8**1

8. 921.**2**823

9. 0.**5**2

DAY 4

Write the value of the underlined number in words

1. 100.48**4**

2. 87.**8**21

3. 731.83**2**

4. 9.1**7**9

5. 82.**7**54

6. **4**.39

7. 925.9**5**76

8. 0.711**5**

9. 93.9**2**

Place value 4

DAY 1

1. 3.1
    + 4.6
    ─────

2. 5.2
    + 4.6
    ─────

3. 1.8
    + 7.1
    ─────

4. 4.74
    + 6.12
    ──────

5. 3.24
    + 5.13
    ──────

6. 2.81
    + 6.46
    ──────

7. Find £5.14 + £6.72.

8. Find 4.623 kg + 3.945 kg.

9. Jamie has £2.72, Ibrahim has £5.24 and Hallie has £7.91. How much do they have altogether?

10. Aisha walked 6.1 km, Sam walked 4.9 km and Fraser walked 7.36 km. How far did they walk in total?

DAY 2

1. 4.2
    + 6.7
    ─────

2. 1.7
    + 4.6
    ─────

3. 2.4
    + 7.3
    ─────

4. 6.26
    + 1.68
    ──────

5. 4.73
    + 3.26
    ──────

6. 2.65
    + 3.92
    ──────

7. Find £63.48 + £14.81.

8. Find 7.488 kg + 5.811 kg.

9. Niall has £7.36, Joe has £8.24 and Freya has £2.85. How much do they have altogether?

10. Alex walked 4.29 km, Sean walked 6.47 km and Shazia walked 5.35 km. How far did they walk in total?

Week 3

DAY 3

1. 6.3 + 5.6
2. 2.6 + 8.8
3. 4.6 + 4.9

4. 8.28 + 9.21
5. 5.76 + 2.35
6. 7.78 + 5.15

7. Find £53.79 + £36.72.

8. Find 7.915 kg + 3.49 kg.

9. Frankie has £6.84, Seamus has £4.99 and Salman has £8.99. How much do they have altogether?

10. Iman walked 3.97 km, Fiona walked 8.7 km and Harry walked 3.05 km. How far did they walk in total?

DAY 4

1. 5.4 + 2.1
2. 8.6 + 9.3
3. 9.3 + 5.7

4. 5.32 + 2.55
5. 3.64 + 7.37
6. 4.93 + 3.74

7. Find £82.29 + £49.35.

8. Find 4.284 kg + 6.909 kg.

9. Jack has £32.62, Abdul has £74.91 and Aneesha has £49.28. How much do they have altogether?

10. Nikita walked 4.95 km, Zara walked 8.3 km and Iain walked 9.97 km. How far did they walk in total?

Addition of decimal numbers   6

DAY 1

1.   8 . 8
   − 2 . 3
   —————

2.   9 . 8
   − 6 . 3
   —————

3.   8 . 7
   − 1 . 9
   —————

4.   4 . 6 5
   − 3 . 1 6
   ——————

5.   6 . 2 7
   − 3 . 1 3
   ——————

6.   9 . 6 3
   − 3 . 2 7
   ——————

7. Find £5.97 − £2.39.

8. Find 6.943 kg − 4.283 kg.

9. A piece of wood is 7.2 m long. Stephen cuts 4.8 m from one end, how long is the piece leftover?

10. Javad has saved £8.45; he spends £2.29 on a comic. How much does he have left?

DAY 2

1.   7 . 7
   − 2 . 7
   —————

2.   7 . 6
   − 2 . 9
   —————

3.   5 . 9
   − 4 . 2
   —————

4.   8 . 6 8
   − 4 . 8 5
   ——————

5.   9 . 3 6
   − 6 . 4 4
   ——————

6.   4 . 2 6
   − 1 . 1 7
   ——————

7. Find £29.41 − £4.29.

8. Find 9.194 kg − 6.78 kg.

9. A piece of rope is 6.8 m long. Julia cuts 4.9 m from one end, how long is the piece leftover?

10. Naomi has £7, she spends £4.82 on sweets. How much does she have left?

7 | **Week 4**

DAY 3

1.
$$\begin{array}{r} 4\ .\ 7 \\ -\ 3\ .\ 6 \\ \hline \end{array}$$

2.
$$\begin{array}{r} 9\ .\ 5 \\ -\ 7\ .\ 8 \\ \hline \end{array}$$

3.
$$\begin{array}{r} 3\ .\ 2 \\ -\ 2\ .\ 9 \\ \hline \end{array}$$

4.
$$\begin{array}{r} 6\ .\ 4\ 6 \\ -\ 1\ .\ 2\ 9 \\ \hline \end{array}$$

5.
$$\begin{array}{r} 9\ .\ 8\ 3 \\ -\ 4\ .\ 4\ 6 \\ \hline \end{array}$$

6.
$$\begin{array}{r} 8\ .\ 1\ 2 \\ -\ 6\ .\ 9\ 6 \\ \hline \end{array}$$

7. Find £3.78 – £2.59.

8. Find 8.937 kg – 0.859 kg.

9. A piece of wood is 3.5 m long. Tyler cuts 2.98 m from one end, how long is the piece leftover?

10. Lara has saved £4.36, she spends £2.89 on a comic. How much does she have left?

DAY 4

1.
$$\begin{array}{r} 7\ .\ 7 \\ -\ 6\ .\ 2 \\ \hline \end{array}$$

2.
$$\begin{array}{r} 3\ .\ 6 \\ -\ 1\ .\ 9 \\ \hline \end{array}$$

3.
$$\begin{array}{r} 9\ .\ 7 \\ -\ 5\ .\ 7 \\ \hline \end{array}$$

4.
$$\begin{array}{r} 8\ .\ 3\ 9 \\ -\ 2\ .\ 7\ 9 \\ \hline \end{array}$$

5.
$$\begin{array}{r} 6\ .\ 6\ 4 \\ -\ 2\ .\ 5\ 5 \\ \hline \end{array}$$

6.
$$\begin{array}{r} 9\ .\ 5\ 2 \\ -\ 7\ .\ 7\ 8 \\ \hline \end{array}$$

7. Find £15.18 - £14.19.

8. Find 5.104 kg – 3.527 kg.

9. A piece of rope is 18 m long. Freya cuts 12.49 m from one end, how long is the piece leftover?

10. Mira has £15, she spends £8.27 on sweets. How much does she have left?

Subtraction of decimal numbers 8

DAY 1

Show working for questions 1-5:

1. 42.84 + 35.16

2. 92.43 – 62.75

3. 83.294 + 98.982

4. 51.8 – 12.794

5. 6.820 + 2.619 + 3.625

6. Order the following numbers from the smallest to the largest:

    (a) 7.857, 8.567, 6.785, 7.685, 6.858, 8.657

    (b) 4.304, 4.044, 4.034, 4.403, 4.344

    (c) 3.602, 3.026, 3.062, 3.226, 3.622, 3.206

DAY 2

Show working for questions 1-5:

1. 59.29 + 34.59

2. 64.92 – 42.87

3. 67.21 + 54.42

4. 79.2 – 32.691

5. 5.2 + 7.132 + 9.09

6. Order the following numbers from the smallest to the largest:

    (a) 6.0606, 6.06, 6.006, 6, 6.066, 6.606

    (b) 80.9, 0.89, 9.08, 8.09, 90.8, 9.8

    (c) 3.337, 3.373, 7.337, 3.737, 3.377, 7.373

Week 5

DAY 3

Show working for questions 1-5:

1. 75.93 + 29.08

2. 187.21 − 77.92

3. 130.29 + 71.83

4. 72 − 58.283

5. 2 + 7.4 + 8.812

6. Order the following numbers from the smallest to the largest:

   (a) 9.319, 9.91, 9.139, 9.913, 9.1953

   (b) 1.111, 1.11, 1.101, 1.001, 1.01

   (c) 7.0707, 7.07, 7.007, 7.077, 7.77, 7

DAY 4

Show working for questions 1-5:

1. 34.62 + 73.17

2. 93.49 − 31.79

3. 45.28 + 172.45

4. 88 − 34.781

5. 6.7 + 1.29 + 5.032

6. Order the following numbers from the smallest to the largest:

   (a) 2.202, 2.022, 2.021, 2.102, 2.012, 2.12

   (b) 0.9559, 0.9505, 0.5995, 0.5599, 0.5959

   (c) 0.974, 49.7, 7.094, 0.947, 490.7, 79.4

Mixed decimals 10

DAY 1

1. Calculate each of the following:
   (a) 5.814+ 2.175
   (b) 7.26 – 5.371
   (c) 4.381 + 15.209

2. Round the following to 1 decimal place:
   (a) 6.78   (b) 9.817   (c) 18.856

3. What does the bold red number represent: 4.**3**28?

4. Order the following numbers in increasing order:
   2.232, 2.332, 2.323, 2.222, 2.322, 2.223, 2.233

5. When Isla was 7 years old, she was 1.31 m tall. Now she is 1.67 m tall. How much has she grown?

6. Harvey has £6.94 and Arjun has £10.75. How much more does Arjun have than Harvey?

DAY 2

1. Calculate each of the following:
   (a) 4.275 + 8.714
   (b) 4.821 – 1.732
   (c) 4.7 – 1.549

2. Round the following to 1 decimal place:
   (a) 3.77   (b) 68.65   (c) 22.951

3. What does the bold red number represent: 1.7**8**7?

4. Order the following numbers in increasing order:
   1.213, 1.312, 1.123, 1.132, 1.231, 1.321

5. When Salman was 5 years old, he was 0.85 m tall. Now he is 1.4 m tall. How much has he grown?

6. Peter has £22.95 and Komel has £59.32. How much more does Komel have than Peter?

11   Week 6

DAY 3

1. Calculate each of the following:
   (a) 3.8 + 5.596
   (b) 4.483 − 0.999
   (c) 7.234 + 45.881

2. Round the following to 1 decimal place:
   (a) 98.744   (b) 6.861   (c) 64.559

3. What does the bold red number represent: 7.3**5**?

4. Order the following numbers in increasing order:
   6.555, 6.578, 6.788, 6.785, 6.575, 6.857, 6.875

5. When Haider was 4 years old, he was 0.73 m tall. Now he is 1.6 m tall. How much has he grown?

6. Alasdair has £48.95 and Gaia has £85.37. How much more does Gaia have than Alasdair?

DAY 4

1. Calculate each of the following:
   (a) 7.283 + 6.959
   (b) 4.9 − 4.832
   (c) 14.772 − 3.864

2. Round the following to 1 decimal place:
   (a) 5.852   (b) 0.65   (c) 9.999

3. What does the bold red number represent: 5.**2**16?

4. Order the following numbers in increasing order:
   9.645, 9.564, 9.465, 9.646, 9.546, 9.544

5. When Laiba was 9 years old, she was 1.03 m tall. Now she is 1.5 m tall. How much has she grown?

6. Gigi has £54.34 and Dowd has £73.86. How much more does Dowd have than Gigi?

Mixed decimals   12

DAY 1

Calculate each of the following (show all working):

1. 0.72 × 2
2. 0.48 × 4
3. 2.74 × 5
4. 5.81 × 6
5. 6.23 × 4
6. 2.04 ÷ 3
7. 7.48 ÷ 4
8. 4.72 ÷ 2
9. 6.85 ÷ 5
10. 8.91 ÷ 9

DAY 2

Calculate each of the following (show all working):

1. 2.23 × 3
2. 1.84 × 4
3. 7.71 × 6
4. 0.95 × 9
5. 15.37 × 2
6. 7.74 ÷ 2
7. 0.64 ÷ 4
8. 4.20 ÷ 5
9. 3.06 ÷ 3
10. 6.36 ÷ 6

Week 7

DAY 3

Calculate each of the following (show all working):

1. 0.91 × 5
2. 1.12 × 8
3. 3.09 × 6
4. 7.86 × 4
5. 5.91 × 9
6. 15.55 ÷ 5
7. 1.92 ÷ 3
8. 2.08 ÷ 4
9. 0.72 ÷ 6
10. 0.96 ÷ 8

DAY 4

Calculate each of the following (show all working):

1. 4.84 × 4
2. 1.13 × 6
3. 0.12 × 5
4. 7.89 × 7
5. 5.90 × 9
6. 9.45 ÷ 3
7. 6.95 ÷ 5
8. 6.24 ÷ 2
9. 8.72 ÷ 8
10. 7.605 ÷ 9

Multiplication and divison of decimal numbers

DAY 1

1. Calculate each of the following:
   (a) 4.1 × 10
   (b) 9.63 × 100
   (c) 0.99 × 1000
   (d) 6.7 × 10
   (e) 1.1 × 100
   (f) 1.59 × 1000

2. Use two-step multiplication to calculate the following:
   (e.g., 2.4 × 20 = (2.4 × 2) × 10 = 4.8 × 10 = 48)
   (a) 5.4 × 20
   (b) 1.5 × 200
   (c) 9.1 × 40
   (d) 3.7 × 50

DAY 2

1. Calculate each of the following:
   (a) 2.7 × 10
   (b) 4.41 × 100
   (c) 0.95 × 1000
   (d) 0.10 × 10
   (e) 0.085 × 100
   (f) 2.094 × 1000

2. Use two-step multiplication to calculate the following:
   (e.g., 0.31 × 30 = (0.31 × 3) × 10 = 0.93 × 10 = 9.3)
   (a) 6.2 × 30
   (b) 5.14 × 300
   (c) 0.74 × 20
   (d) 1.12 × 200

Week 8

DAY 3

1. Calculate each of the following:

    (a) 7.4×10

    (b) 3.13×100

    (c) 61.28×1000

    (d) 114.8×10

    (e) 0.51×100

    (f) 8.92×1000

2. Use two-step multiplication to calculate the following:
(e.g., $1.6 \times 20 = (1.6 \times 2) \times 10 = 0.8 \times 10 = 0.08$)

    (a) 4.3×20

    (b) 6.12×300

    (c) 0.7×30

    (d) 6.8×500

DAY 4

1. Calculate each of the following:

    (a) 8.1×10

    (b) 3.9×100

    (c) 1.99×1000

    (d) 0.87×10

    (e) 9.99×100

    (f) 4.50×1000

2. Use two-step multiplication to calculate the following:
(e.g., $0.23 \times 40 = (0.23 \times 4) \times 10 = 0.92 \times 10 = 9.2$)

    (a) 5.72×20

    (b) 1.11×200

    (c) 0.5×50

    (d) 7.8×70

Multiply decimals by multiples of 10, 100 and 1000

DAY 1

1. Calculate each of the following:
   (a) 4.1 ÷ 10
   (b) 8.9 ÷ 100
   (c) 653 ÷ 1000
   (d) 3.27 ÷ 10
   (e) 7.92 ÷ 100
   (f) 34.1 ÷ 1000

2. Use two-step division to calculate the following:
   (e.g., 1.6 ÷ 20 = (1.6 ÷ 2) ÷ 10 = 0.8 ÷ 10 = 0.08)
   (a) 4.2 ÷ 20
   (b) 56.2 ÷ 200
   (c) 2.7 ÷ 30
   (d) 1.5 ÷ 50

DAY 2

1. Calculate each of the following:
   (a) 5.91 ÷ 10
   (b) 37.3 ÷ 100
   (c) 82.5 ÷ 1000
   (d) 71.4 ÷ 10
   (e) 82.8 ÷ 100
   (f) 72.83 ÷ 1000

2. Use two-step division to calculate the following:
   (e.g., 3.2 ÷ 40 = (3.2 ÷ 4) ÷ 10 = 0.8 ÷ 10 = 0.08)
   (a) 3.6 ÷ 20
   (b) 642 ÷ 200
   (c) 36 ÷ 40
   (d) 1.8 ÷ 300

Week 9

DAY 3

1. Calculate each of the following:
   - (a) 67.2 ÷ 10
   - (b) 5.93 ÷ 100
   - (c) 824.6 ÷ 1000
   - (d) 72.8 ÷ 10
   - (e) 82.37 ÷ 100
   - (f) 726.1 ÷ 1000

2. Use two-step division to calculate the following:
   (e.g., 4.5 ÷ 500 = (4.5 ÷ 5) ÷ 100 = 0.9 ÷ 100 = 0.009)
   - (a) 34.6 ÷ 20
   - (b) 5.24 ÷ 200
   - (c) 25 ÷ 50
   - (d) 7.2 ÷ 60

DAY 4

1. Calculate each of the following:
   - (a) 7.31 ÷ 10
   - (b) 4.28 ÷ 100
   - (c) 45.89 ÷ 1000
   - (d) 0.82 ÷ 10
   - (e) 0.618 ÷ 100
   - (f) 43.21 ÷ 1000

2. Use two-step division to calculate the following:
   (e.g., 56 ÷ 80 = (56 ÷ 8) ÷ 10 = 7 ÷ 10 = 0.7)
   - (a) 62 ÷ 20
   - (b) 312 ÷ 200
   - (c) 4.8 ÷ 40
   - (d) 7 ÷ 70

Divide decimals by multiples of 10, 100 and 1000

DAY 1

1. Copy and complete each of the following:

   (a) $\dfrac{1}{2}$ of £6 (b) $\dfrac{1}{4}$ of £32

   (c) $\dfrac{1}{2}$ of £48 (d) $\dfrac{1}{4}$ of £4

   (e) $\dfrac{1}{3}$ of £24 (f) $\dfrac{1}{3}$ of £300

2. Copy and complete each of the following:
   (e.g., $\dfrac{3}{4}$ of £40 = 40 ÷ 4 × 3 = £30)

   (a) $\dfrac{3}{4}$ of 24 g (b) $\dfrac{1}{2}$ of 70 m

   (c) $\dfrac{2}{3}$ of £36 (d) $\dfrac{2}{3}$ of 48 kg

   (e) $\dfrac{3}{4}$ of 60 km (f) $\dfrac{3}{4}$ of 36p

DAY 2

1. Copy and complete each of the following:

   (a) $\dfrac{1}{10}$ of £40 (b) $\dfrac{1}{5}$ of £100

   (c) $\dfrac{1}{4}$ of £80 (d) $\dfrac{1}{10}$ of £50

   (e) $\dfrac{1}{5}$ of £40 (f) $\dfrac{1}{4}$ of £28

2. Copy and complete each of the following:
   (e.g., $\dfrac{2}{5}$ of £40 = 40 ÷ 5 × 2 = £16)

   (a) $\dfrac{3}{10}$ of 400 g (b) $\dfrac{3}{4}$ of 20 m

   (c) $\dfrac{2}{5}$ of £55 (d) $\dfrac{3}{5}$ of 45 kg

   (e) $\dfrac{2}{3}$ of 27 km (f) $\dfrac{4}{5}$ of 40p

Week 10

DAY 3

1. Copy and complete each of the following:

(a) $\frac{1}{4}$ of £60

(b) $\frac{1}{3}$ of £39

(c) $\frac{1}{5}$ of £35

(d) $\frac{1}{10}$ of £50

(e) $\frac{1}{6}$ of £48

(f) $\frac{1}{6}$ of £36

2. Copy and complete each of the following:
(e.g., $\frac{7}{10}$ of £40 = 40 ÷ 10 × 7 = £28)

(a) $\frac{2}{3}$ of 24 g

(b) $\frac{3}{5}$ of 10 m

(c) $\frac{3}{4}$ of £84

(d) $\frac{9}{10}$ of 60 kg

(e) $\frac{4}{5}$ of 35 km

(f) $\frac{5}{6}$ of 42p

DAY 4

1. Copy and complete each of the following:

(a) $\frac{1}{5}$ of £70

(b) $\frac{1}{10}$ of £80

(c) $\frac{1}{8}$ of £56

(d) $\frac{1}{6}$ of £36

(e) $\frac{1}{20}$ of £60

(f) $\frac{1}{5}$ of £35

2. Copy and complete each of the following:
(e.g., $\frac{5}{8}$ of £40 = 40 ÷ 8 × 5 = £25)

(a) $\frac{3}{4}$ of 52 g

(b) $\frac{4}{5}$ of 100 m

(c) $\frac{7}{20}$ of £40

(d) $\frac{5}{6}$ of 72 kg

(e) $\frac{9}{10}$ of 70 km

(f) $\frac{3}{8}$ of 64p

Fractions of a quantity   20

DAY 1

1. Copy and complete each of the following:

   (a) $\frac{2}{3}$ of £36   (b) $\frac{1}{10}$ of £70

   (c) $\frac{3}{5}$ of £75   (d) $\frac{3}{4}$ of £88

   (e) $\frac{1}{3}$ of £24   (f) $\frac{3}{7}$ of £35

2. Sam and Eva buy a pizza to share; the pizza costs £24. Eva eats three quarters of the pizza. How much does Eva need to pay?

3. A school has 560 pupils; two fifths of the pupils are girls. How many pupils are girls?

4. A car weighs 650 kg; three tenths of the weight of the car is metal. What weight of metal is in the car?

When you see a calculator on the page, you may use one for the exercise.

DAY 2

1. Copy and complete each of the following:

   (a) $\frac{3}{4}$ of £40   (b) $\frac{5}{7}$ of £28

   (c) $\frac{1}{6}$ of £42   (d) $\frac{4}{5}$ of £90

   (e) $\frac{1}{2}$ of £54   (f) $\frac{2}{3}$ of £24

2. Clovis and Morag buy a cake to share; the cake costs £9. Clovis ea[ts] cake. How much does Clovis need to pay?

3. A company owns 96 cars; three quarters of them are blue. How many cars are blue?

4. A chocolate bar weighs 60 g; three fifths of the bar is sugar. How much sugar is in the chocolate bar?

21   Week 11

DAY 3

1. Copy and complete each of the following:

   (a) $\frac{1}{7}$ of £56

   (b) $\frac{2}{5}$ of £75

   (c) $\frac{7}{10}$ of £90

   (d) $\frac{3}{4}$ of £100

   (e) $\frac{3}{7}$ of £42

   (f) $\frac{1}{3}$ of £33

2. Charles and Kamila buy some sweets to share; the sweets cost £15. Charles eats four fifths of the sweets. How much does Charles need to pay?

3. A school has 352 pupils; three eighths of the pupils are boys. How many pupils are boys?

4. A car weighs 1400 kg; three quarters of the weight of the car is metal. What weight of metal is in the car?

DAY 4

1. Copy and complete each of the following:

   (a) $\frac{1}{3}$ of £27

   (b) $\frac{3}{5}$ of £40

   (c) $\frac{5}{8}$ of £72

   (d) $\frac{2}{9}$ of £81

   (e) $\frac{1}{4}$ of £36

   (f) $\frac{5}{6}$ of £42

2. Leonardo and Izzy buy a cake to share; the cake costs £5.40. Izzy eats five ninths of the cake. How much should Izzy pay?

3. A company owns 124 cars; one quarter of them are red. How many cars are red?

4. A chocolate bar weighs 56 g; two sevenths of the bar is sugar. How much sugar is in the chocolate bar?

Fractions of a quantity 22

DAY 1

1. Write three equivalent fractions for each of the following:

   (a) $\dfrac{2}{3}$ (b) $\dfrac{1}{2}$ (c) $\dfrac{3}{4}$

2. Simplify each of the following by dividing the numerator and denominator by the same number:

   (a) $\dfrac{4}{8}$ (b) $\dfrac{3}{9}$ (c) $\dfrac{2}{10}$

3. For each of the following statements, write out the fraction in its simplest form:

   (a) Four days of a week.

   (b) Six months of a year.

   (c) Nine days of September.

   (d) Twenty days of a year (not a leap year).

DAY 2

1. Write three equivalent fractions for each of the following:

   (a) $\dfrac{1}{10}$ (b) $\dfrac{2}{5}$ (c) $\dfrac{3}{7}$

2. Simplify each of the following by dividing the numerator and denominator by the same number:

   (a) $\dfrac{3}{24}$ (b) $\dfrac{9}{12}$ (c) $\dfrac{6}{8}$

3. For each of the following statements, write out the fraction in its simplest form:

   (a) Two days of a week.

   (b) Four months of a year.

   (c) Fourteen days of February (not a leap year).

   (d) Ten days of a year (not a leap year).

23 Week 12

DAY 3

1. Write three equivalent fractions for each of the following:
   (a) $\dfrac{1}{3}$ (b) $\dfrac{5}{8}$ (c) $\dfrac{3}{10}$

2. Simplify each of the following by dividing the numerator and denominator by the same number:
   (a) $\dfrac{25}{30}$ (b) $\dfrac{14}{21}$ (c) $\dfrac{40}{100}$

3. For each of the following statements, write out the fraction in its simplest form:

   (a) Five days of a week.

   (b) Nine months of a year.

   (c) Three days of April.

   (d) Five days of a year (not a leap year).

DAY 4

1. Write three equivalent fractions for each of the following:
   (a) $\dfrac{4}{5}$ (b) $\dfrac{1}{6}$ (c) $\dfrac{3}{7}$

2. Simplify each of the following by dividing the numerator and denominator by the same number:
   (a) $\dfrac{9}{12}$ (b) $\dfrac{7}{70}$ (c) $\dfrac{12}{36}$

3. For each of the following statements, write out the fraction in its simplest form:

   (a) Seven days of a week.

   (b) Five months of a year.

   (c) Twelve days of August.

   (d) Ninety days of a year (not a leap year).

Mixed fractions questions 24

DAY 1

1. Put the following fractions in order from smallest to largest:
   $\frac{1}{4}, \frac{2}{3}, \frac{1}{5}, \frac{1}{2}$

2. Change the following improper fractions to mixed numbers:
   (a) $\frac{3}{2}$ (b) $\frac{34}{10}$ (c) $\frac{16}{3}$

3. Change the following mixed numbers to improper fractions:
   (a) $2\frac{2}{3}$ (b) $5\frac{3}{4}$ (c) $1\frac{4}{5}$

4. In a school car park there are 60 cars. One fifth of the cars are white, one quarter are red and one tenth are black. The rest are silver, what fraction are silver?

DAY 2

1. Put the following fractions in order from smallest to largest:
   $\frac{7}{10}, \frac{1}{3}, \frac{3}{4}, \frac{2}{5}$

2. Change the following improper fractions to mixed numbers:
   (a) $\frac{43}{5}$ (b) $\frac{31}{9}$ (c) $\frac{26}{4}$

3. Change the following mixed numbers to improper fractions:
   (a) $8\frac{3}{10}$ (b) $3\frac{5}{6}$ (c) $5\frac{4}{9}$

4. On a school bus there are 90 pupils. One third of the pupils are twelve years old, one sixth are eleven and one fifth are ten. The rest are nine, what fraction are nine?

Week 13

DAY 3

1. Put the following fractions in order from smallest to largest:

$$\frac{2}{3}, \frac{4}{5}, \frac{1}{2}, \frac{1}{6}$$

2. Change the following improper fractions to mixed numbers:

(a) $\frac{45}{8}$ (b) $\frac{28}{3}$ (c) $\frac{64}{6}$

3. Change the following mixed numbers to improper fractions:

(a) $5\frac{3}{10}$ (b) $2\frac{1}{5}$ (c) $7\frac{7}{8}$

4. In a school car park there are 72 cars. One third of the cars are white, one sixth are red and one eighth are black. The rest are silver, what fraction are silver?

DAY 4

1. Put the following fractions in order from smallest to largest:

$$\frac{11}{20}, \frac{7}{8}, \frac{1}{6}, \frac{3}{5}$$

2. Change the following improper fractions to mixed numbers:

(a) $\frac{43}{12}$ (b) $\frac{27}{6}$ (c) $\frac{63}{5}$

3. Change the following mixed numbers to improper fractions:

(a) $7\frac{3}{4}$ (b) $1\frac{5}{12}$ (c) $12\frac{7}{9}$

4. On a school bus there are 96 pupils. One quarter of the pupils are twelve years old, one half are eleven and one eighth are ten. The rest are nine, what fraction are nine?

Mixed fractions questions 26

DAY 1

1. By making the denominator 100, change the following fractions into percentages:
   (a) $\frac{1}{4}$
   (b) $\frac{3}{5}$
   (c) $\frac{7}{10}$

2. By making the denominator 10, 100 or 1000, change the following fractions into decimals:
   (a) $\frac{3}{25}$
   (b) $\frac{7}{20}$
   (c) $\frac{41}{50}$

3. Change the following percentages into fractions and simplify:
   (a) 60%
   (b) 15%
   (c) 72%

4. Change the following decimals into percentages and simplified fractions:
   (a) 0.8
   (b) 1.5
   (c) 0.35

DAY 2

1. By making the denominator 100, change the following fractions into percentages:
   (a) $\frac{1}{25}$
   (b) $\frac{4}{5}$
   (c) $\frac{7}{20}$

2. By making the denominator 10, 100 or 1000, change the following fractions into decimals:
   (a) $\frac{9}{50}$
   (b) $\frac{2}{5}$
   (c) $\frac{24}{25}$

3. Change the following percentages into fractions and simplify:
   (a) 5%
   (b) 28%
   (c) 55%

4. Change the following decimals into percentages and simplified fractions:
   (a) 0.75
   (b) 0.01
   (c) 0.9

27   Week 14

DAY 3

1. By making the denominator 100, change the following fractions into percentages:
   (a) $\frac{9}{10}$ (b) $\frac{3}{4}$ (c) $\frac{1}{20}$

2. By making the denominator 10, 100 or 1000, change the following fractions into decimals:
   (a) $\frac{11}{50}$ (b) $\frac{9}{10}$ (c) $\frac{18}{25}$

3. Change the following percentages into fractions and simplify:
   (a) 81%   (b) 1%   (c) 15%

4. Change the following decimals into percentages and simplified fractions:
   (a) 0.07   (b) 0.68   (c) 1.25

DAY 4

1. By making the denominator 100, change the following fractions into percentages:
   (a) $\frac{3}{40}$ (b) $\frac{4}{20}$ (c) $\frac{15}{4}$

2. By making the denominator 10, 100 or 1000, change the following fractions into decimals:
   (a) $\frac{6}{500}$ (b) $\frac{2}{25}$ (c) $\frac{7}{200}$

3. Change the following percentages into fractions and simplify:
   (a) 42%   (b) 180%   (c) 2.9%

4. Change the following decimals into percentages and simplified fractions:
   (a) 0.09   (b) 0.55   (c) 0.2

Fractions, decimals & percentages

DAY 1

1. Change the following into percentages and decimals:

   (a) $\frac{5}{25}$ (b) $\frac{1}{10}$ (c) $\frac{3}{4}$

2. Change the following into simplified fractions and percentages:

   (a) 0.25   (b) 0.9   (c) 0.11

3. Change the following into decimals and simplified fractions:

   (a) 48%   (b) 80%   (c) 1%

4. Which is greater, 0.25 or $\frac{1}{5}$? Give a reason for your answer.

DAY 2

1. Change the following into percentages and decimals:

   (a) $\frac{2}{5}$ (b) $\frac{9}{20}$ (c) $\frac{4}{50}$

2. Change the following into simplified fractions and percentages:

   (a) 0.88   (b) 0.03   (c) 0.35

3. Change the following into decimals and simplified fractions:

   (a) 66%   (b) 10%   (c) 45%

4. Which is greater, 0.35 or $\frac{9}{20}$? Give a reason for your answer.

DAY 3

1. Change the following into percentages and decimals:

   (a) $\dfrac{1}{50}$　　　(b) $\dfrac{4}{5}$　　　(c) $\dfrac{5}{25}$

2. Change the following into simplified fractions and percentages:

   (a) 0.9　　　(b) 0.65　　　(c) 0.05

3. Change the following into decimals and simplified fractions:

   (a) 15%　　　(b) 92%　　　(c) 70%

4. Which is greater, 0.71 or $\dfrac{3}{4}$? Give a reason for your answer.

DAY 4

1. Change the following into percentages and decimals:

   (a) $\dfrac{7}{10}$　　　(b) $\dfrac{3}{5}$　　　(c) $\dfrac{10}{200}$

2. Change the following into simplified fractions and percentages:

   (a) 0.75　　　(b) 0.01　　　(c) 0.4

3. Change the following into decimals and simplified fractions:

   (a) 78%　　　(b) 20%　　　(c) 2%

4. Which is greater, 0.12 or $\dfrac{1}{20}$? Give a reason for your answer.

Fractions, decimals & percentages 30

DAY 1

1. Calculate each of the following:

    (a) 10% of £28
    (b) 20% of £30
    (c) 5% of £400
    (d) 50% of £200
    (e) 1% of £73
    (f) 25% of £500

2. By adding together simple percentages, find the following:

    (a) 20% of £60
    (b) 40% of £24
    (c) 15% of £80
    (d) 30% of £250

DAY 2

1. Calculate each of the following:

    (a) 10% of £95
    (b) 20% of £48
    (c) 5% of £40
    (d) 50% of £60
    (e) 1% of £4
    (f) 25% of £12

2. By adding together simple percentages, find the following:

    (a) 15% of £50
    (b) 90% of £72
    (c) 70% of £35
    (d) 55% of £380

DAY 3

1. Calculate each of the following:

    (a) 10% of £3
    (b) 20% of £45
    (c) 5% of £68
    (d) 50% of £98
    (e) 1% of £29
    (f) 25% of £48

2. By adding together simple percentages, find the following:

    (a) 55% of £10
    (b) 20% of £48
    (c) 11% of £20
    (d) 50% of £5

DAY 4

1. Calculate each of the following:

    (a) 10% of £27
    (b) 20% of £64
    (c) 5% of £92
    (d) 50% of £75
    (e) 1% of £6
    (f) 25% of £200

2. By adding together simple percentages, find the following:

    (a) 5% of £65
    (b) 20% of £32
    (c) 55% of £50
    (d) 60% of £45

Percentages of a quantity

DAY 1

1. Using a calculator, calculate each of the following:

    (a) 13% of 263 kg
    (b) 98% of 5.9 ml
    (c) 42% of 729 cm
    (d) 74% of £38

2. A clothes shop has a 25% sale. Calculate the sale price of a jumper which normally costs £45.

3. Hana went on a diet and lost 18% of her body weight. Before dieting Hana weighed 125 kg, how much does she now weigh?

4. In a maths test Muhammad scored 85%. If the test was out of 20 marks, what did Muhammad score?

DAY 2

1. Using a calculator, calculate each of the following:

    (a) 27% of 56 kg
    (b) 85% of 99 ml
    (c) 9% of 246 cm
    (d) 65% of £48

2. A clothes shop has a 30% sale. Calculate the sale price of a jacket which normally costs £55.

3. Faris went on a diet and lost 15% of his weight. Before dieting Faris weighed 140 kg, how much does he now weigh?

4. In a maths test Iona scored 70%. If the test was out of 80 marks, what did Iona score?

33 Week 17

DAY 3

1. Using a calculator, calculate each of the following:

    (a) 21% of 16 kg
    (b) 1% of 42 ml
    (c) 84% of 3 cm
    (d) 51% of £81

2. A clothes shop has a 15% sale. Calculate the sale price of a jumper which normally costs £70.

3. Joe went on a diet and lost 9% of his weight. Before dieting Joe weighed 68 kg, how much does he now weigh?

4. In a maths test Josefina scored 75%. If the test was out of 60 marks, what did Josefina score?

DAY 4

1. Using a calculator, calculate each of the following:

    (a) 8% of 67 kg
    (b) 64% of 3 ml
    (c) 2% of 2550 cm
    (d) 42% of £6

2. A clothes shop has a 40% sale. Calculate the sale price of a jumper which normally costs £36.

3. Anna went on a diet and lost 21% of her weight. Before dieting Anna weighed 95 kg, how much does she now weigh?

4. In a maths test Ali scored 90%. If the test was out of 40 marks, what did Ali score?

Percentages of a quantity 34

DAY 1

1. Write out each of the following as a fraction, a decimal and a percentage: (e.g., $0.4 = \frac{4}{10} = \frac{2}{5} = 40\%$)

   (a) $\frac{1}{4}$ (b) 65%   (c) 0.4

2. In a survey, a group of 240 school pupils were asked their favourite football team. Of those asked 35% said Dundee United, 10% Aberdeen, 30% Hibernian and 25% Hearts. How many of those asked said:
   (a) Dundee United   (b) Hibernian   (c) Hearts ?

3. In another survey 150 pupils were asked what pets they have. Of those asked, 0.3 have a cat, one fifth have a dog and 16% have more than one pet. How many have:
   (a) a dog   (b) a cat   (c) more than one pet ?

DAY 2

1. Write out each of the following as a fraction, a decimal and a percentage: (e.g., $0.4 = \frac{4}{10} = \frac{2}{5} = 40\%$)

   (a) $\frac{7}{20}$ (b) 32%   (c) 0.88

2. In a survey, a group of 300 school pupils were asked their favourite football team. Of those asked 24% said Rangers, 23% Celtic, 20% Partick Thistle and 33% Motherwell. How many of those asked said:
   (a) Rangers   (b) Celtic   (c) Motherwell ?

3. Four friends shared a pizza. Rachel ate 35%, Asif ate 0.2 and Frankie ate one quarter. What percentage did Jordan eat?

35 Week 18

DAY 3

1. Write out each of the following as a fraction, a decimal and a percentage: (e.g., $0.4 = \frac{4}{10} = \frac{2}{5} = 40\%$)

   (a) $\frac{4}{5}$ (b) 3%   (c) 0.32

2. In a survey, a group of 500 school pupils were asked their favourite football team. Of those asked 23% said Dundee United, 25% Aberdeen, 28% Hibernian and the rest Hearts. How many of those asked said:

   (a) Dundee United   (b) Hibernian   (c) Hearts ?

3. In another survey, 280 pupils were asked what pets they have. Of those asked, 0.45 said have a cat, one quarter have a dog and 15% have more than one pet. How many have:

   (a) a dog   (b) a cat   (c) more than one pet ?

DAY 4

1. Write out each of the following as a fraction, a decimal and a percentage: (e.g., $0.4 = \frac{4}{10} = \frac{2}{5} = 40\%$)

   (a) $\frac{11}{20}$ (b) 99%   (c) 0.02

2. In a survey, a group of 120 school pupils were asked their favourite football team. Of those asked 30% said Rangers, 35% Celtic, 20% Partick Thistle and the rest Motherwell. How many of those asked said:

   (a) Rangers   (b) Celtic   (c) Motherwell ?

3. Four friends shared a pizza. Jasmine ate 15%, Oscar ate 0.25 and Qasim ate one fifth. What percentage did Reia eat?

Fractions, decimals & percentages   36

DAY 1

1. Convert the following lengths:
   (a) 72 cm to mm
   (b) 26 cm to m
   (c) 1.3 m to cm
   (d) 86 m to mm
   (e) 4721 m to km
   (f) 59 km to m

2. Convert the following weights:
   (a) 11 kg to g
   (b) 3952 g to kg
   (c) 568 g to kg

3. Convert the following volumes:
   (a) 34 litres to ml
   (b) 670 ml to litres

DAY 2

1. Convert the following lengths:
   (a) 45 cm to mm
   (b) 61 cm to m
   (c) 3.2 m to cm
   (d) 5 m to mm
   (e) 225 m to km
   (f) 3 km to m

2. Convert the following weights:
   (a) 2 kg to g
   (b) 3450 g to kg
   (c) 92 g to kg

3. Convert the following volumes:
   (a) 6 litres to ml
   (b) 725 ml to litres

Week 19

DAY 3

1. Convert the following lengths:
   - (a) 5.6 cm to mm
   - (b) 591 cm to m
   - (c) 0.7 m to cm
   - (d) 2 m to mm
   - (e) 624 m to km
   - (f) 9.9 km to m

2. Convert the following weights:
   - (a) 14 kg to g
   - (b) 792 g to kg
   - (c) 54 g to kg

3. Convert the following volumes:
   - (a) 6 litres to ml
   - (b) 45 ml to litres

DAY 4

1. Convert the following lengths:
   - (a) 2 cm to mm
   - (b) 629 cm to m
   - (c) 0.7 m to cm
   - (d) 0.2 m to mm
   - (e) 51 m to km
   - (f) 0.08 km to m

2. Convert the following weights:
   - (a) 17 kg to g
   - (b) 308 g to kg
   - (c) 42 g to kg

3. Convert the following volumes:
   - (a) 0.5 litres to ml
   - (b) 82ml to litres

Unit conversions

DAY 1

Simplify these expressions by collecting like terms:

1. $a - a + a$

2. $b + b - b - b$

3. $c + c + c - c$

4. $d - d + d + d$

5. $e - e + e + e - e$

6. $a - b + a + b$

7. $b + c + c - b$

8. $3 \times a + 4 \times b$

9. $a + a + a \times 3$ (Careful!)

DAY 2

Simplify these expressions by collecting like terms:

1. $a + a + a - a + a$

2. $b + b + b + b + b + b + b$

3. $c + c + c - c - c$

4. $d + d + d + d + d$

5. $e - e + e + e - e - e$

6. $a + b - a + a + b + b + a$

7. $b + c - c + b + c + b$

8. $5 \times a + 2 \times b$

9. $a - a + a + a \times 5$ (Careful!)

DAY 3

Simplify these expressions by collecting like terms:

1. $a + a + a + a + a + a + a + a$

2. $b + b + b - b + b$

3. $c - c - c + c + c + c - c + c$

4. $d - d + d - d - d + d + d$

5. $e - e - e + e + e$

6. $a + a + b + a + a - b + a$

7. $c + c + b - c + b + b - c - b$

8. $9 \times a + 3 \times b$

9. $a - a - a + a \times 4$ (Careful!)

DAY 4

Simplify these expressions by collecting like terms:

1. $a - a + a - a + a - a - a + a$

2. $b + b - b - b + b$

3. $c - c + c - c + c - c$

4. $d + d - d + d - d$

5. $e - e + e + e - e + e$

6. $a + a + a - a + b - a + b$

7. $a + b + c + a - b - c$

8. $5 \times a + 6 \times b$

9. $a + a + a + a - a \times 4$ (Careful!)

Simplifying expressions 40

DAY 1

Simplify these expressions by collecting like terms:

1. $5a + 2a + 7a - 8a$

2. $4b + 5b + 16b + 30b$

3. $9c - 5c - 3c + 9c$

4. $2d - d + 5d + 3d$

5. $9e - 6e - e + 5e$

6. $7a + b - 5a + 4b$

7. $7b + 8c + b - 7c$

8. $6c + 4d - 3c - 3d$

9. $3d + 6e + 5 - d + 6e + 9$

DAY 2

Simplify these expressions by collecting like terms:

1. $a + 5a + 8a - a$

2. $12b + 4b + b + 3b$

3. $10c - 7c - 2c + 8c$

4. $18d - 4d + d - 9d$

5. $e + 6e - 5e + 2e$

6. $19a + 11b - 15a + 10b$

7. $31b + 5c - 12b - c$

8. $64c + 40d - 25c + 19d$

9. $18d + 32e + 15 - 7d + e - 12$

DAY 3

Simplify these expressions by collecting like terms:

1. $5a + 17a - a - 9a$
2. $6b + b + 7b + 52b$
3. $39c - 12c - c - 15c$
4. $75d - 48d + 22d - 32d$
5. $30e + 29e - 35e + 17e$
6. $14a + 7b - 11a + 8b$
7. $26b + 45c + 7b - 11c$
8. $150c + 120d - 80c - 65d$
9. $45d + 37e + 18 - 38d - 24e + 27$

DAY 4

Simplify these expressions by collecting like terms:

1. $6a + 9a + a - 10a$
2. $7b - 3b + 4b + 21b$
3. $25c - 15c - c + 12c$
4. $27d - 14d + 31d - 26d$
5. $18e - 5e - 9e + 6e$
6. $48a + 12b + 24a - 8b$
7. $39b + 27c - 13b + 27c$
8. $90c + 200d - 140d - 65c$
9. $52d + 45e + 32 + 9d - 41e - 27$

Simplifying expressions

DAY 1

Solve the following equations:

1. $x + 2 = 8$
2. $x - 5 = 3$
3. $x + 4 = 6$
4. $x + 22 = 27$
5. $x + 6 = 24$
6. $x - 12 = 11$
7. $x + 24 = 54$
8. $x - 9 = 4$

DAY 2

Solve the following equations:

1. $x + 3 = 4$
2. $x - 5 = 12$
3. $x - 6 = 17$
4. $x + 2 = 12$
5. $x - 15 = 61$
6. $x + 9 = 21$
7. $x + 54 = 72$
8. $x - 8 = 9$

DAY 3

Solve the following equations:

1. $x + 7 = 21$
2. $x - 7 = 53$
3. $x + 6 = 6$
4. $x + 64 = 90$
5. $x - 5 = 43$
6. $x - 21 = 73$
7. $x + 54 = 59$
8. $x + 12 = 32$

DAY 4

Solve the following equations:

1. $x + 1 = 43$
2. $x - 5 = 26$
3. $x - 14 = 18$
4. $x + 43 = 79$
5. $x + 8 = 23$
6. $x - 7 = 34$
7. $x + 54 = 61$
8. $x - 6 = 57$

DAY 1

Solve the following equations:

1. $2x = 18$
2. $4x = 40$
3. $5x = 25$
4. $3x = 24$
5. $7x = 350$
6. $9x = 63$
7. $6x = 18$
8. $11x = 44$

DAY 2

Solve the following equations:

1. $4x = 16$
2. $7x = 14$
3. $3x = 36$
4. $5x = 100$
5. $9x = 54$
6. $6x = 90$
7. $10x = 250$
8. $12x = 96$

DAY 3

Solve the following equations:

1. $7x = 28$
2. $4x = 80$
3. $8x = 56$
4. $5x = 120$
5. $9x = 108$
6. $3x = 15$
7. $20x = 160$
8. $50x = 250$

DAY 4

Solve the following equations:

1. $8x = 48$
2. $4x = 44$
3. $2x = 14$
4. $9x = 27$
5. $10x = 1500$
6. $3x = 48$
7. $15x = 75$
8. $40x = 280$

Solving equations

DAY 1

Solve the following equations:

1. 3x + 4 = 10
2. 4x − 6 = 34
3. 9x + 2 = 20
4. 5x + 15 = 35
5. 7x + 6 = 41
6. 6x − 15 = 21
7. 8x + 9 = 65
8. 3x − 4 = 32

DAY 2

Solve the following equations:

1. 5x + 6 = 41
2. 4x − 8 = 8
3. 7x + 9 = 23
4. 8x + 12 = 36
5. 2x + 5 = 29
6. 3x − 6 = 27
7. 9x + 11 = 38
8. 11x − 7 = 37

Week 24

DAY 3

Solve the following equations:

1. 6x + 12 = 42
2. 3x – 6 = 18
3. 5x + 4 = 59
4. 9x + 7 = 61
5. 8x + 13 = 45
6. 12x – 7 = 17
7. 7x + 3 = 80
8. 15x + 11 = 101

DAY 4

Solve the following equations:

1. 6x + 8 = 62
2. 9x – 4 = 86
3. 8x + 3 = 27
4. 30x + 35 = 155
5. 17x + 36 = 121
6. 7x – 9 = 26
7. 12x - 23 = 109
8. 20x – 25 = 95

DAY 1

1. Find the next three terms in each sequence:
   (a) 12, 17, 22
   (b) 2, 14, 26
   (c) 26, 34, 42
   (d) 22, 32, 42

2. For each of the tables below, find the 4th and 5th numbers:
   (a)
A	1	2	3	4	5
B	6	10	14		

   (b)
C	1	2	3	4	5
D	2	5	8		

3. For each of the tables in question 2, find a rule that connects A to B and C to D.

4. Draw the next pattern:

   A   B   C

DAY 2

1. Find the next three terms in each sequence:
   (a) 9, 15, 21
   (b) 41, 54, 67
   (c) 23, 30, 37
   (d) 15, 26, 37

2. For each of the tables below, find the 4th and 5th numbers:
   (a)
A	1	2	3	4	5
B	5	13	21		

   (b)
C	1	2	3	4	5
D	8	18	28		

3. For each of the tables in question 2, find a rule that connects A to B and C to D.

4. Draw the next pattern:

   A   B   C

Week 25

DAY 3

1. Find the next three terms in each sequence:
   (a) 9, 18, 27
   (b) 15, 22, 29
   (c) 3, 12, 21
   (d) 5, 11, 17

2. For each of the tables below, find the 4th and 5th numbers:
   (a)
A	1	2	3	4	5
B	6	11	16		

   (b)
C	1	2	3	4	5
D	16	28	40		

3. For each of the tables in question 2, find a rule that connects A to B and C to D.

4. Draw the next pattern:

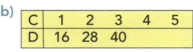

A   B   C

DAY 4

1. Find the next three terms in each sequence:
   (a) 47, 51, 55
   (b) 112, 119, 126
   (c) 150, 180, 210
   (d) 0.2, 0.5, 0.8

2. For each of the tables below, find the 4th and 5th numbers:
   (a)
A	1	2	3	4	5
B	7	16	25		

   (b)
C	1	2	3	4	5
D	8	15	22		

3. For each of the tables in question 2, find a rule that connects A to B and C to D.

4. Draw the next pattern:

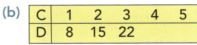

A   B   C

Patterns & sequences   50

DAY 1

1. Find the area of the following shapes (show working):

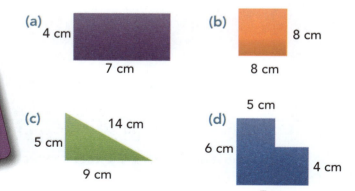

2. Find the perimeter of each of the above shapes.

DAY 2

1. Find the area of the following shapes (show working):

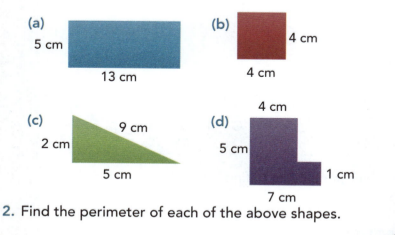

2. Find the perimeter of each of the above shapes.

Week 26

DAY 3

1. Find the area of the following shapes (show working):

(a)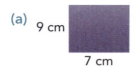

(b)

(c)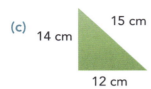

(d)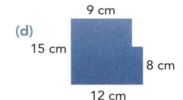

2. Find the perimeter of each of the above shapes.

DAY 4

1. Find the area of the following shapes (show working):

(a)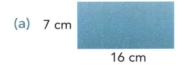

(b)

(c) (d)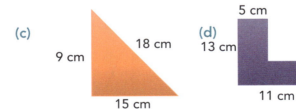

2. Find the perimeter of each of the above shapes.

Area & perimeter

DAY 1

1. Name the type of angle:

   (a)

   (b)

2. Give a definition of each of your answers to question 1.

3. Calculate the missing angle in the following questions:

   (a)

   (b)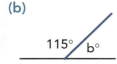

4. Olivia is facing west. If she turns 45° clockwise, what direction is she now facing?

DAY 2

1. Name the type of angle:

   (a)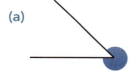

   (b)

2. Give a definition of each of your answers to question 1.

3. Calculate the missing angle in the following questions:

   (a)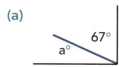

   (b)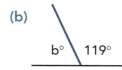

4. Muiz is facing south-west. If he turns 90° anti-clockwise, what direction is he now facing?

Week 27

DAY 3

1. Name the type of angle:

   (a)    (b)

2. Give a definition of each of your answers to question 1.

3. Calculate the missing angle in the following questions:

   (a)   (b)

4. Zachary is facing east. If he turns 135° anti-clockwise, what direction is he now facing?

DAY 4

1. Name the type of angle:

   (a) 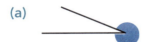   (b)

2. Give a definition of each of your answers to question 1.

3. Calculate the missing angle in the following questions:

   (a)   (b)

4. Heidi is facing south-west. If she turns 90° clockwise, what direction is she now facing?

Angles 54

DAY 1

1. Find 429.4 × 4.

2. Solve: $x - 7 = 8$.

3. Find 54 × 600.

4. Find 55% of 1200 kg.

5. Find $\frac{3}{4}$ of 892.

6. Simplify: $5a + 2a - 4a$.

7. Find 8351 − 6834.

8. Find the mean of 4, 5, 2, 6, 3.

9. How many cm are there in 38.40 m?

10. What is the complement of 17°?

DAY 2

1. Find 627.5 × 9.

2. Solve: $x - 11 = 19$.

3. Find 49 × 400.

4. Find 15% of 48 kg.

5. Find $\frac{3}{4}$ of 208.

6. Simplify: $4a - 3a + a$.

7. Find 5832 − 4922.

8. Find the mean of 10, 13, 8, 12, 7.

9. How many mm are there in 6.4 m?

10. What is the supplement of 39°?

55 **Week 28**

DAY 3

1. Find 245.9 × 7.

2. Solve: $x - 4 = 17$.

3. Find 45.84 × 500.

4. Find 11% of 3200 kg.

5. Find $\frac{3}{4}$ of 312.

6. Simplify: $a + 4a - 3a$.

7. Find 8468 − 5732.

8. Find the mean of 8, 11, 7, 6.

9. How many cm are there in 53.2 m?

10. What is the complement of 56°?

DAY 4

1. Find 538.7 × 9.

2. Solve: $x - 15 = 23$.

3. Find 62.79 × 400.

4. Find 22% of 600 kg.

5. Find $\frac{3}{4}$ of 876.

6. Simplify: $5a - 4a + 2a$.

7. Find 7395 − 3552.

8. Find the mean of 7, 9, 6, 8, 10, 8.

9. How many mm are there in 56.3 m?

10. What is the supplement of 42°?

Mixed exercise 56

DAY 1

1. Find $7576 \div 8$.

2. Solve: $6x = 48$.

3. Find $724.1 \div 100$.

4. Find the area of the rectangle.

   9 cm
   14 cm

5. Change 740 mm to cm.

6. Put the following numbers in order from the smallest to the largest: -76, 54, 24, 82, 25, -49

7. Find 225×5.

8. Describe an acute angle.

DAY 2

1. Find $3348 \div 9$.

2. Solve: $9x = 81$.

3. Find $64.6 \div 100$.

4. Find the area of the triangle.

   7 cm
   12 cm

5. Change 450 mm to m.

6. Put the following numbers in order from the smallest to the largest: 87, -91, 0, 27, -3, -28

7. Find 628×4.

8. Describe an obtuse angle.

DAY 3

1. Find 14961 ÷ 3.
2. Solve: $11x = 132$.
3. Find 956.2 ÷ 100.
4. Find the area of the square.
5. Change 672 cm to mm.
6. Put the following numbers in order from the smallest to the largest: 44, 12, -55, -8, 53, 43
7. Find 657 × 3.
8. Describe a right angle.

12 cm

DAY 4

1. Find 6006 ÷ 7.
2. Solve: $6x = 42$.
3. Find 735.7 ÷ 100.
4. Find the area of the shape.
5. Change 1120 mm to cm.
6. Put the following numbers in order from the smallest to the largest: -101, 0, -1, 98, -42, -87
7. Find 482 × 7.
8. Describe a reflex angle.

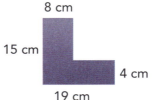
8 cm
15 cm
4 cm
19 cm

Mixed exercise   58

DAY 1

1. Calculate the volume of the cuboid:

   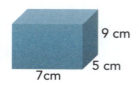

2. Solve $6x = 42$.
3. Solve $2x - 5 = 7$.
4. Find 3.21×6.
5. Simplify $\dfrac{20}{80}$.
6. Find $2 + 3 \times (2 + 2)$.
7. Write down all the factors of 12.
8. Simplify $2a + 3a + 3a - 7a$.
9. Find $\dfrac{1}{3}$ of £96.

DAY 2

1. Calculate the volume of the cube:

2. Solve $x - 6 = 15$.
3. Solve $3x - 1 = 8$.
4. Find $12.84 \div 6$.
5. Simplify $\dfrac{16}{40}$.
6. Find $9 + 3 \div (6 - 4)$.
7. Write down all the factors of 8.
8. Simplify $a + 2a - a + 3a$.
9. Find $\dfrac{2}{5}$ of £50.

Week 30

DAY 3

1. Calculate the volume of the cuboid: :

   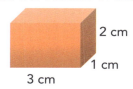

2. Solve $3x = 42$.

3. Solve $3x - 2 = 22$.

4. Find 1.21×6.

5. Simplify $\frac{28}{84}$.

6. Find $6 + 3 \times (3 + 5)$.

7. Write down all the factors of 27.

8. Simplify $2a + 6a - a + a$.

9. Find $\frac{3}{4}$ of £32.

DAY 4

1. Calculate the volume of the cube:

2. Solve $x + 9 = 15$.

3. Solve $5x - 6 = 24$.

4. Find $12.88 \div 7$.

5. Simplify $\frac{42}{49}$.

6. Find $4 + 20 \div (7 - 5)$.

7. Write down all the factors of 24.

8. Simplify $5a - 7a + 3a$.

9. Find $\frac{2}{7}$ of £63.

Mixed exercise

ANSWERS

Week 1

Day 1
1. (a) 7.1 (b) 2.8 (c) 1.5
   (d) 2.5 (e) 63.9 (f) 29.9
2. (a) 4.19 (b) 9.25 (c) 1.49
   (d) 7.02 (e) 87.70 (f) 99.49
3. (a) £24 (b) £48
   (c) £72 (d) £28

Day 2
1. (a) 17.4 (b) 8.9 (c) 63.9
   (d) 58.4 (e) 27.9 (f) 143.0
2. (a) 6.93 (b) 1.68 (c) 21.94
   (d) 48.75 (e) 71.96 (f) 238.00
3. (a) £24 (b) £27
   (c) £200 (d) £70

Day 3
1. (a) 6.6 (b) 4.2 (c) 9.3
   (d) 2.8 (e) 14.7 (f) 72.1
2. (a) 2.76 (b) 0.84 (c) 15.73
   (d) 52.72 (e) 0.71 (f) 121.24
3. (a) £8 (b) £4
   (c) £250 (d) £90

Day 4
1. (a) 7.5 (b) 4.3 (c) 0.1
   (d) 63.8 (e) 81.9 (f) 53.0
2. (a) 9.80 (b) 4.29 (c) 21.46
   (d) 8.25 (e) 101.19 (f) 90.00
3. (a) £20 (b) £30
   (c) £45 (d) £27

Week 2

Day 1
1. One hundredth
2. Seven tenths
3. Six thousandths
4. Two hundredths
5. One unit
6. Nine tenths
7. Five thousandths
8. Seven thousandths
9. Eight hundredths

Day 2
1. Two units
2. Five hundredths
3. Eight thousandths
4. Three tenths
5. Nine tens
6. One tenth
7. Seven hundredths
8. Five ten thousandths
9. Three tenths

Day 3
1. Six tenths
2. Two thousandths
3. One ten
4. Four hundredths
5. Nine units
6. Six thousandths
7. Eight thousandths
8. Two tenths
9. Five tenths

Day 4
1. Four thousandths
2. Eight tenths
3. Two thousandths
4. Seven hundredths
5. Seven tenths
6. Four units
7. Five hundredths
8. Five ten thousandths
9. Two hundredths

Week 3

Day 1
1. 7.7 2. 9.8 3. 8.9
4. 10.86 5. 8.37 6. 9.27
7. £11.86 8. 8.568 kg 9. £15.87
10. 18.36 km

Day 2
1. 10.9 2. 6.3 3. 9.7
4. 7.94 5. 7.99 6. 6.57
7. £78.29 8. 13.299 kg 9. £18.45
10. 16.11 km

Day 3
1. 11.9 2. 11.4 3. 9.5
4. 17.49 5. 8.11 6. 12.93
7. £90.51 8. 11.405 kg 9. £20.82
10. 15.72 km

Day 4
1. 7.5 2. 17.9 3. 15.0
4. 7.87 5. 11.01 6. 8.67
7. £131.64 8. 11.193 kg 9. £156.81
10. 23.22 km

Week 4

Day 1
1. 6.5 2. 3.5 3. 6.8
4. 1.49 5. 3.14 6. 6.36
7. £3.58 8. 2.66 kg 9. 2.4 m
10. £6.16

Day 2
1. 5 2. 4.7 3. 1.7
4. 3.83 5. 2.92 6. 3.09
7. £25.12 8. 2.414 kg 9. 1.9 m
10. £2.18

Day 3
1. 1.1 2. 1.7 3. 0.3
4. 5.17 5. 5.37 6. 1.16
7. £1.19 8. 8.078 kg 9. 0.52 m
10. £1.47

Day 4
1. 1.5 2. 1.7 3. 4.0
4. 5.60 5. 4.09 6. 1.74
7. £0.99 8. 1.577 kg 9. 5.51 m
10. £6.73

Week 5

Day 1
1. 78 2. 29.68 3. 182.276
4. 39.006 5. 13.064
6. (a) 6.785, 6.858, 7.685, 7.857, 8.567, 8.6
   (b) 4.034, 4.044, 4.304, 4.344, 4.403
   (c) 3.026, 3.062, 3.206, 3.226, 3.602, 3.6

Day 2
1. 93.88 2. 22.05 3. 121.63
4. 46.509 5. 21.422
6. (a) 6, 6.006, 6.06, 6.0606, 6.066, 6.606
   (b) 0.89, 8.09, 9.08, 9.8, 80.9, 90.8
   (c) 3.337, 3.373, 3.377, 3.737, 7.337, 7.3

Day 3
1. 105.01 2. 109.29 3. 202.12
4. 13.717 5. 18.212
6. (a) 9.139, 9.1953, 9.319, 9.91, 9.913
   (b) 1.001, 1.010, 1.101, 1.11, 1.111
   (c) 7, 7.007, 7.07, 7.0707, 7.077, 7.77

Day 4
1. 107.79 2. 61.7 3. 217.73
4. 53.219 5. 13.022
6. (a) 2.012, 2.021, 2.022, 2.102, 2.120, 2.20
   (b) 0.5599, 0.5959, 0.5995, 0.9505, 0.955
   (c) 0.947, 0.974, 7.094, 49.70, 79.40, 490

Week 6

Day 1
1. (a) 7.989   (b) 1.889   (c) 19.59
2. (a) 6.8   (b) 9.8   (c) 18.9
3. Three tenths
4. 2.222, 2.223, 2.232, 2.233, 2.322, 2.323, 2.332
5. 0.36 m   6. £3.81

Day 2
1. (a) 12.989   (b) 3.089   (c) 3.151
2. (a) 3.8   (b) 68.7   (c) 23.0
3. Eight hundredths
4. 1.123, 1.132, 1.213, 1.231, 1.312, 1.321
5. 0.55 m   6. £36.37

Day 3
1. (a) 9.396   (b) 3.484   (c) 53.115
2. (a) 98.7   (b) 6.9   (c) 64.6
3. Five hundredths
4. 6.555, 6.575, 6.578, 6.785, 6.788, 6.857, 6.875
5. 0.87 m   6. £36.42

Day 4
1. (a) 14.242   (b) 0.058   (c) 10.908
2. (a) 5.9   (b) 0.7   (c) 10.0
3. Two tenths
4. 9.465, 9.544, 9.546, 9.564, 9.645, 9.646
5. 0.47 m   6. £19.52

Week 7

Day 1
1. 1.44   2. 1.92   3. 13.7
4. 34.86   5. 24.92   6. 0.68
7. 1.87   8. 2.36   9. 1.37
10. 0.99

Day 2
1. 6.69   2. 7.36   3. 46.26
4. 8.55   5. 30.74   6. 3.87
7. 0.16   8. 0.84   9. 1.02
10. 1.06

Day 3
1. 4.55   2. 8.96   3. 18.54
4. 31.44   5. 53.19   6. 3.11
7. 0.64   8. 0.52   9. 0.12
10. 0.12

Day 4
1. 19.36   2. 6.78   3. 0.6
4. 55.23   5. 53.1   6. 3.15
7. 1.39   8. 3.12   9. 1.09

---

10. 0.845

Week 8

Day 1
1. (a) 41   (b) 963   (c) 990
   (d) 67   (e) 110   (f) 1590
2. (a) 108   (b) 300
   (c) 364   (d) 185

Day 2
1. (a) 27   (b) 441   (c) 950
   (d) 1   (e) 8.5   (f) 2094
2. (a) 186   (b) 1542
   (c) 14.8   (d) 224

Day 3
1. (a) 74   (b) 313   (c) 61280
   (d) 1148   (e) 51   (f) 8920
2. (a) 86   (b) 1836
   (c) 21   (d) 3400

Day 4
1. (a) 81   (b) 390   (c) 1990
   (d) 8.7   (e) 999   (f) 4500
2. (a) 114.4   (b) 222
   (c) 25   (d) 546

Week 9

Day 1
1. (a) 0.41   (b) 0.089   (c) 0.653
   (d) 0.327   (e) 0.0792   (f) 0.0341
2. (a) 0.21   (b) 0.281
   (c) 0.09   (d) 0.03

Day 2
1. (a) 0.591   (b) 0.373   (c) 0.0825
   (d) 7.14   (e) 0.828   (f) 0.07283
2. (a) 0.18   (b) 3.21
   (c) 0.9   (d) 0.006

Day 3
1. (a) 6.72   (b) 0.0593   (c) 0.8246
   (d) 7.28   (e) 0.8237   (f) 0.7261
2. (a) 1.73   (b) 0.0262
   (c) 0.5   (d) 0.12

Day 4
1. (a) 0.731   (b) 0.0428   (c) 0.04589
   (d) 0.082   (e) 0.00618   (f) 0.04321
2. (a) 3.1   (b) 1.56
   (c) 0.12   (d) 0.1

Week 10

Day 1
1. (a) £3   (b) £8   (c) £24
   (d) £1   (e) £8   (f) £100
2. (a) 18 g   (b) 35 m   (c) £24
   (d) 32 kg   (e) 45 km   (f) 27p

Day 2
1. (a) £4   (b) £20   (c) £20
   (d) £12   (e) £48   (f) £7
2. (a) 120 g   (b) 15 m   (c) £22
   (d) 27 kg   (e) 18 km   (f) 32p

Day 3
1. (a) £15   (b) £13   (c) £7
   (d) £5   (e) £8   (f) £6
2. (a) 16 g   (b) 6 m   (c) £63
   (d) 54 kg   (e) 28 km   (f) 35p

Day 4
1. (a) £14   (b) £8   (c) £7
   (d) £6   (e) £3   (f) £7
2. (a) 39 g   (b) 80 m   (c) £14
   (d) 60 kg   (e) 63 km   (f) 24p

Week 11

Day 1
1. (a) £24   (b) £7   (c) £45
   (d) £66   (e) £8   (f) £15
2. £18   3. 224 pupils   4. 195 kg

Day 2
1. (a) £30   (b) £20   (c) £7
   (d) £72   (e) £27   (f) £16
2. £6   3. 72 cars   4. 36 g

Day 3
1. (a) £8   (b) £30   (c) £63
   (d) £75   (e) £18   (f) £11
2. £12   3. 132 pupils   4. 1050 kg

Day 4
1. (a) £9   (b) £24   (c) £45
   (d) £18   (e) £9   (f) £35
2. £3   3. 31 cars   4. 16 g

Week 12

Day 1
1. (a) any three, e.g. $\frac{4}{6} = \frac{6}{9} = \frac{8}{12} = \cdots$
   (b) any three, e.g. $\frac{2}{4} = \frac{3}{6} = \frac{4}{8} = \cdots$
   (c) any three, e.g. $\frac{6}{8} = \frac{9}{12} = \frac{12}{16} = \cdots$
2. (a) $\frac{1}{2}$ (b) $\frac{1}{3}$ (c) $\frac{1}{5}$
3. (a) $\frac{4}{7}$ (b) $\frac{1}{2}$

62

(c) $\frac{3}{10}$ (d) $\frac{4}{73}$

Day 2
1. (a) any three, e.g. $\frac{2}{20} = \frac{3}{30} = \frac{10}{100} = \cdots$
   (b) any three, e.g. $\frac{4}{10} = \frac{10}{25} = \frac{20}{50} = \cdots$
   (c) any three, e.g. $\frac{6}{14} = \frac{9}{21} = \frac{12}{28} = \cdots$
2. (a) $\frac{1}{8}$ (b) $\frac{3}{4}$ (c) $\frac{3}{4}$
3. (a) $\frac{2}{7}$ (b) $\frac{1}{3}$
   (c) $\frac{1}{2}$ (d) $\frac{2}{73}$

Day 3
1. (a) any three, e.g. $\frac{2}{3} = \frac{3}{9} = \frac{10}{15} = \cdots$
   (b) any three, e.g. $\frac{10}{16} = \frac{20}{32} = \frac{25}{40} = \cdots$
   (c) any three, e.g. $\frac{6}{20} = \frac{9}{30} = \frac{12}{40} = \cdots$
2. (a) $\frac{5}{6}$ (b) $\frac{2}{3}$ (c) $\frac{2}{5}$
3. (a) $\frac{5}{7}$ (b) $\frac{3}{4}$
   (c) $\frac{1}{10}$ (d) $\frac{1}{73}$

Day 4
1. (a) any three, e.g. $\frac{8}{10} = \frac{20}{25} = \frac{40}{50} = \cdots$
   (b) any three, e.g. $\frac{2}{12} = \frac{5}{30} = \frac{10}{60} = \cdots$
   (c) any three, e.g. $\frac{6}{14} = \frac{18}{42} = \frac{27}{63} = \cdots$
2. (a) $\frac{3}{4}$ (b) $\frac{1}{10}$ (c) $\frac{1}{3}$
3. (a) 1   (b) $\frac{5}{12}$
   (c) $\frac{12}{31}$ (d) $\frac{18}{73}$

Week 13
Day 1
1. $\frac{1}{5}, \frac{1}{4}, \frac{1}{2}, \frac{2}{3}$
2. (a) $1\frac{1}{2}$ (b) $3\frac{2}{5}$ (c) $5\frac{1}{3}$
3. (a) $\frac{8}{3}$ (b) $\frac{23}{4}$ (c) $\frac{9}{5}$
4. $\frac{9}{20}$

Day 2
1. $\frac{1}{3}, \frac{2}{5}, \frac{7}{10}, \frac{3}{4}$
2. (a) $8\frac{3}{5}$ (b) $3\frac{4}{9}$ (c) $6\frac{1}{2}$
3. (a) $\frac{83}{10}$ (b) $\frac{23}{6}$ (c) $\frac{49}{9}$
4. $\frac{3}{10}$

Day 3
1. $\frac{1}{6}, \frac{1}{2}, \frac{2}{3}, \frac{4}{5}$
2. (a) $5\frac{5}{8}$ (b) $9\frac{1}{3}$ (c) $10\frac{2}{3}$
3. (a) $\frac{53}{10}$ (b) $\frac{11}{5}$ (c) $\frac{63}{8}$
4. $\frac{3}{8}$

Day 4
1. $\frac{1}{6}, \frac{11}{20}, \frac{3}{5}, \frac{7}{8}$
2. (a) $3\frac{7}{12}$ (b) $4\frac{1}{2}$ (c) $12\frac{3}{5}$
3. (a) $\frac{31}{4}$ (b) $\frac{17}{12}$ (c) $\frac{115}{9}$
4. $\frac{1}{8}$

Week 14
Day 1
1. (a) 25%   (b) 60%   (c) 70%
2. (a) 0.12   (b) 0.35   (c) 0.82
3. (a) $\frac{3}{5}$ (b) $\frac{3}{20}$ (c) $\frac{18}{25}$
4. (a) $80\% = \frac{4}{5}$
   (b) $150\% = \frac{3}{2}$
   (c) $35\% = \frac{7}{20}$

Day 2
1. (a) 4%   (b) 80%   (c) 35%
2. (a) 0.18   (b) 0.4   (c) 0.96
3. (a) $\frac{1}{20}$ (b) $\frac{7}{25}$ (c) $\frac{11}{20}$
4. (a) $75\% = \frac{3}{4}$
   (b) $1\% = \frac{1}{100}$
   (c) $90\% = \frac{9}{10}$

Day 3
1. (a) 90%   (b) 75%   (c) 5%
2. (a) 0.22   (b) 0.9   (c) 0.72
3. (a) $\frac{81}{100}$ (b) $\frac{1}{100}$ (c) $\frac{3}{20}$
4. (a) $7\% = \frac{7}{100}$
   (b) $68\% = \frac{17}{25}$
   (c) $125\% = \frac{5}{4}$

Day 4
1. (a) 7.5%   (b) 20%   (c) 375%
2. (a) 0.012   (b) 0.08   (c) 0.035
3. (a) $\frac{21}{50}$ (b) $\frac{9}{5}$ (c) $\frac{29}{1000}$
4. (a) $9\% = \frac{9}{100}$
   (b) $55\% = \frac{11}{20}$
   (c) $20\% = \frac{1}{5}$

Week 15
Day 1
1. (a) 20% = 0.2   (b) 10% = 0.1
   (c) 75% = 0.75
2. (a) $\frac{1}{4} = 25\%$ (b) $\frac{9}{10} = 90\%$
   (c) $\frac{11}{100} = 11\%$
3. (a) $0.48 = \frac{12}{25}$ (b) $0.8 = \frac{4}{5}$
   (c) $0.01 = \frac{1}{100}$
4. 0.25 is greater

Day 2
1. (a) 40% = 0.4   (b) 45% = 0.45
   (c) 8% = 0.08
2. (a) $\frac{22}{25} = 88\%$ (b) $\frac{3}{100} = 3\%$
   (c) $\frac{7}{20} = 35\%$
3. (a) $0.66 = \frac{33}{50}$ (b) $0.1 = \frac{1}{10}$
   (c) $0.45 = \frac{9}{20}$
4. $\frac{9}{20}$ is greater

Day 3
1. (a) 2% = 0.02   (b) 80% = 0.8
   (c) 20% = 0.2
2. (a) $\frac{9}{10} = 90\%$ (b) $\frac{13}{20} = 65\%$
   (c) $\frac{1}{20} = 5\%$
3. (a) $0.15 = \frac{3}{20}$ (b) $0.92 = \frac{23}{25}$
   (c) $0.7 = \frac{7}{10}$
4. $\frac{3}{4}$ is greater

Day 4
1. (a) 70% = 0.7   (b) 60% = 0.6
   (c) 5% = 0.05
2. (a) $\frac{3}{4} = 75\%$ (b) $\frac{1}{100} = 1\%$
   (c) $\frac{2}{5} = 40\%$
3. (a) $0.78 = \frac{39}{50}$ (b) $0.2 = \frac{1}{5}$
   (c) $0.02 = \frac{1}{50}$
4. 0.12 is greater

Week 16
Day 1
1. (a) £2.80   (b) £6   (c) £20
   (d) £100   (e) £0.73   (f) £125
2. (a) £12   (b) £9.60
   (c) £12   (d) £75

Day 2
1. (a) £9.50   (b) £9.60   (c) £2
   (d) £30   (e) £0.04   (f) £3
2. (a) £7.50   (b) £64.80
   (c) £24.50   (d) £209

Day 3
1. (a) £0.30   (b) £9   (c) £3.40
   (d) £49   (e) £0.29   (f) £12
2. (a) £5.50   (b) £9.60
   (c) £2.20   (d) £2.50

Day 4
1. (a) £2.70   (b) £12.80   (c) £4.60
   (d) £37.50   (e) £0.06   (f) £50

(a) £3.25   (b) £6.40
(c) £27.50   (d) £27

Week 17
Day 1
(a) 34.19 kg   (b) 5.782 ml
(c) 306.18 cm   (d) £28.12
£33.75   3. 102.5 kg
17 marks

Day 2
(a) 15.12 kg   (b) 84.15 ml
(c) 22.14 cm   (d) £31.20
£38.50   3. 119 kg
56 marks

Day 3
(a) 3.36 kg   (b) 0.42 ml
(c) 2.52 cm   (d) £41.31
£59.50   3. 61.88 kg
45 marks

Day 4
(a) 5.36 kg   (b) 1.92 ml
(c) 51cm   (d) £2.52
£21.60   3. 75.05 kg
36 marks

Week 18
Day 1
(a) $\frac{1}{4} = 0.25 = 25\%$
(b) $\frac{13}{20} = 0.65 = 65\%$
(c) $\frac{2}{5} = 0.4 = 40\%$

(a) 84 pupils   (b) 72 pupils   (c) 60 pupils

(a) 30 pupils   (b) 45 pupils   (c) 24 pupils

Day 2
(a) $\frac{7}{20} = 0.35 = 35\%$
(b) $\frac{8}{25} = 0.32 = 32\%$
(c) $\frac{22}{25} = 0.88 = 88\%$
(a) 72 pupils
(b) 69 pupils
(c) 99 pupils
3. 20%

Day 3
(a) $\frac{4}{5} = 0.8 = 80\%$
(b) $\frac{3}{100} = 0.03 = 3\%$
(c) $\frac{8}{25} = 0.32 = 32\%$
2. (a) 115 pupils

(b) 140 pupils
(c) 120 pupils

3. (a) 70 pupils
(b) 126 pupils
(c) 42 pupils

Day 4
1. (a) $\frac{11}{20} = 0.55 = 55\%$
(b) $\frac{99}{100} = 0.99 = 99\%$
(c) $\frac{1}{50} = 0.02 = 2\%$
2. (a) 36 pupils
(b) 42 pupils
(c) 18 pupils
3. 40%

Week 19
Day 1
1.
(a) 720 mm   (b) 0.26 m   (c) 130 cm
(d) 86 000 mm   (e) 4.721 km   (f) 59 000 m
2.
(a) 11 000 g   (b) 3.952 kg   (c) 0.568 kg
3.
(a) 34 000 ml   (b) 0.67 litres

Day 2
1.
(a) 450 mm   (b) 0.61 m   (c) 320 cm
(d) 5000 mm   (e) 0.225 km   (f) 3000 m
2.
(a) 2000 g   (b) 3.45 kg   (c) 0.092 kg
3.
(a) 6000 ml   (b) 0.725 litres

Day 3
1.
(a) 56 mm   (b) 0.591 m   (c) 70 cm
(d) 2000 mm   (e) 0.624 km   (f) 9900 m
2.
(a) 14 000 g   (b) 0.792 kg   (c) 0.054 kg
3.
(a) 6000 ml   (b) 0.045 litres

Day 4
1.
(a) 20 mm   (b) 6.29 m   (c) 70 cm
(d) 200 mm   (e) 0.051 km   (f) 80 m
2.
(a) 17 000 g   (b) 0.308 kg   (c) 0.042 kg
3.
(a) 500 ml   (b) 0.082 litres

Week 20
Day 1
1. a 2. 0   3. $2c$
4. $2d$ 5. e 6. $2a$
7. $2c$ 8. $3a + 4b$ 9. $5a$

Day 2
1. $3a$ 2. $7b$ 3. c
4. $5d$ 5. 0   6. $2a + 3b$
7. $3b + c$ 8. $5a + 2b$ 9. $6a$

Day 3
1. $8a$ 2. $3b$ 3. $2c$
4. d 5. e 6. $5a$
7. $2b$ 8. $9a + 3b$ 9. $3a$

Day 4
1. 0   2. b 3. 0
4. d 5. $2e$ 6. $a + 2b$
7. $2a$ 8. $5a + 6b$ 9. 0

Week 21
Day 1
1. $6a$ 2. $55b$ 3. $10c$
4. $9d$ 5. $7e$ 6. $2a + 5b$
7. $8b + c$ 8. $3c + d$
9. $2d + 12e + 14$

Day 2
1. $13a$ 2. $20b$ 3. $9c$
4. $6d$ 5. $4e$ 6. $4a + 21b$
7. $19b + 4c$ 8. $39c + 59d$
9. $11d + 33e + 3$

Day 3
1. $12a$ 2. $66b$ 3. $11c$
4. $17d$ 5. $41e$ 6. $3a + 15b$
7. $33b + 34c$ 8. $70c + 55d$ 9. $7d + 13e + 45$

Day 4
1. $6a$ 2. $29b$ 3. $21c$
4. $18d$ 5. $10e$ 6. $72a + 4b$
7. $26b + 54c$ 8. $25c + 60d$ 9. $61d + 4e + 5$

Week 22
Day 1
1. $x = 6$ 2. $x = 8$ 3. $x = 2$
4. $x = 5$ 5. $x = 18$ 6. $x = 23$
7. $x = 30$ 8. $x = 13$

Day 2
1. $x = 1$ 2. $x = 17$ 3. $x = 23$
4. $x = 10$ 5. $x = 76$ 6. $x = 12$
7. $x = 18$ 8. $x = 17$

64

Day 3
1. $x = 14$ 2. $x = 60$ 3. $x = 0$
4. $x = 26$ 5. $x = 48$ 6. $x = 94$
7. $x = 5$ 8. $x = 20$

Day 4
1. $x = 42$ 2. $x = 31$ 3. $x = 32$
4. $x = 36$ 5. $x = 15$ 6. $x = 41$
7. $x = 7$ 8. $x = 63$

Week 23
Day 1
1. $x = 9$ 2. $x = 10$ 3. $x = 5$
4. $x = 8$ 5. $x = 50$ 6. $x = 7$
7. $x = 3$ 8. $x = 4$

Day 2
1. $x = 4$ 2. $x = 2$ 3. $x = 12$
4. $x = 20$ 5. $x = 6$ 6. $x = 15$
7. $x = 25$ 8. $x = 8$

Day 3
1. $x = 4$ 2. $x = 20$ 3. $x = 7$
4. $x = 24$ 5. $x = 12$ 6. $x = 5$
7. $x = 8$ 8. $x = 5$

Day 4
1. $x = 6$ 2. $x = 11$ 3. $x = 7$
4. $x = 3$ 5. $x = 150$ 6. $x = 16$
7. $x = 5$ 8. $x = 7$

Week 24
Day 1
1. $x = 2$ 2. $x = 10$ 3. $x = 2$
4. $x = 4$ 5. $x = 5$ 6. $x = 6$
7. $x = 7$ 8. $x = 12$

Day 2
1. $x = 7$ 2. $x = 4$ 3. $x = 2$
4. $x = 3$ 5. $x = 12$ 6. $x = 11$
7. $x = 3$ 8. $x = 4$

Day 3
1. $x = 5$ 2. $x = 8$ 3. $x = 11$
4. $x = 6$ 5. $x = 4$ 6. $x = 2$
7. $x = 11$ 8. $x = 6$

Day 4
1. $x = 9$ 2. $x = 10$ 3. $x = 3$
4. $x = 4$ 5. $x = 5$ 6. $x = 5$
7. $x = 11$ 8. $x = 6$

Week 25
Day 1
1. (a) 27, 32, 37   (b) 38, 50, 62
   (c) 50, 58, 66   (d) 52, 62, 72
2. (a) 18, 22   (b) 11, 14
3. (a) $B = 4A + 2$ (b) $D = 3C - 1$
4.

Day 2
1. (a) 27, 33, 39   (b) 80, 93, 106
   (c) 44, 51, 58   (d) 48, 59, 70
2. (a) 29, 37   (b) 38, 48
3. (a) $B = 8A - 3$ (b) $D = 10C - 2$
4.

Day 3
1. (a) 36, 45, 54   (b) 36, 43, 50
   (c) 30, 39, 48   (d) 23, 29, 35
2. (a) 21, 26   (b) 52, 64
3. (a) $B = 5A + 1$ (b) $D = 12C + 4$
4.

Day 4
1. (a) 59, 63, 67   (b) 133, 140, 147
   (c) 240, 270, 300 (d) 1.1, 1.4, 1.7
2. (a) 34, 43   (b) 29, 36
3. (a) $B = 9A - 2$ (b) $D = 7C + 1$
4.

Week 26
Day 1
1. (a) 28 cm^2 (b) 64 cm^2
   (c) 22.5 cm^2 (d) 38 cm^2
2. (a) 22 cm   (b) 32 cm
   (c) 28 cm   (d) 26 cm

Day 2
1. (a) 65 cm^2 (b) 16 cm^2
   (c) 5 cm^2 (d) 23 cm^2
2. (a) 36 cm   (b) 16 cm
   (c) 16 cm   (d) 24 cm

Day 3
1. (a) 63 cm^2 (b) 144 cm^2
   (c) 84 cm^2 (d) 159 cm^2
2. (a) 32 cm   (b) 48 cm
   (c) 41 cm   (d) 54 cm

Day 4
1. (a) 112 cm^2 (b) 81 cm^2
   (c) 67.5 cm^2 (d) 83 cm^2
2. (a) 46 cm   (b) 36 cm
   (c) 42 cm   (d) 48 cm

Week 27
Day 1
1. (a) An acute angle
   (b) A straight angle
2. (a) Less than 90°
   (b) 180°
3. (a) 38°   (b) 65°
4. North-West

Day 2
1. (a) A reflex angle
   (b) A right angle
2. (a) Greater than 180° and less than 360°
   (b) 90°
3. (a) 23°   (b) 61°
4. South-East

Day 3
1. (a) An obtuse angle
   (b) An acute angle
2. (a) Greater than 90° and less than 180°
   (b) Less than 90°
3. (a) 69°   (b) 86°
4. North-West

Day 4
1. (a) A reflex angle
   (b) A straight angle
2. (a) Greater than 180° and less than 360°
   (b) 180°
3. (a) 52°   (b) 121°
4. North-West

Week 28
Day 1
1. 1717.6   2. $x = 15$ 3. 32 400
4. 660 kg   5. 669   6. $3a$
7. 1517   8. 4   9. 3840 cm
10. 73°

Day 2
1. 5647.5   2. $x = 30$ 3. 19 600
4. 7.2 kg   5. 156   6. $2a$
7. 910   8. 10   9. 6400 mm
10. 51°

Day 3
1. 1721.3   2. $x = 21$ 3. 22 920
4. 352 kg   5. 234   6. $2a$

6   **8.** 8   **9.** 5320 cm

8.3   **2.** $x = 38$ **3.** 25116
kg   **5.** 657   **6.** $3a$
3   **8.** 8   **9.** 56 300 mm
°

29

2. $x = 8$ **3.** 7.241
cm2   **5.** 74 cm
-49, 24, 25, 54, 82
25
angle that measures less than 90°

2
2   **2.** $x = 9$ **3.** 0.646
cm2   **5.** 0.45 m
-28, -3, 0, 27, 87
12
angle that measures greater than 90°
ess than 180°

3
87   **2.** $x = 12$ **3.** 9.562
4 cm^2 **5.** 6720 mm
5, -8, 12, 43, 44, 53
71
angle that measures 90°

4
8   **2.** $x = 7$ **3.** 7.357
4 cm^2 **5.** 112 cm
01, -87, -42, -1, 0, 98,
574
angle that measures greater than 180°
less than 360°

k 30
1
15 cm^3 **2.** $x = 7$ **3.** $x = 6$
9.26   **5.** $\frac{1}{4}$ **6.** 14
2, 3, 4, 6, 12

32

2
cm^3 **2.** $x = 21$ **3.** $x = 3$
.14   **5.** $\frac{2}{5}$ **6.** 11
2, 4, 8
a

---

9. £20

Day 3
1. 6 cm^3 **2.** $x = 14$ **3.** $x = 8$
4. 7.26   **5.** $\frac{1}{3}$ **6.** 30
7. 1, 3, 9, 27
8. $8a$
9. £24

Day 4
1. 64 cm^3 **2.** $x = 6$ **3.** $x = 6$
4. 1.84   **5.** $\frac{6}{7}$ **6.** 14
7. 1, 2, 3, 4, 6, 8, 12, 24
8. a
9. £18